MAIN BATTLE TANKS

The M1A1 Abrams

By Michael and Gladys Green

Consultant:

James M. Warford MAJ, U.S. Army (Retired)

Capstone
press

Mankato, Minnesota

Edge Books are published by Capstone Press
151 Good Counsel Drive, P.O. Box 669, Mankato, Minnesota 56002
http://www.capstonepress.com

Library of Congress Cataloging-in-Publication Data
Green, Michael, 1952–
    Main battle tanks: the M1A1 Abrams / by Michael and Gladys Green.
    p. cm.—(Edge books. War machines)
    Summary: Describes the M1A1 Abrams tank, including its history, equipment,
weapons, tactics, and future use with the U.S. Army.
    Includes bibliographical references and index.
    ISBN 0-7368-2416-2 (hardcover)
    1. M1 (Tank)—Juvenile literature. [1. M1 (Tank) 2. Tanks (Military science)]
I. Green, Gladys, 1954– II. Title. III. Series.
UG446.5.G6934 2004
623.7'4752'0973—dc22   2003012219

Editorial Credits
Carrie Braulick, editor; Jason Knudson, designer; Jo Miller, photo researcher

Photo Credits
Getty Images Inc./AFP/Ahmad Al-Rubaye, 27; AFP/Romeo Gacad, 15;
    Robert Nickelsberg, 23; Scott Nelson, 9
Photo by Ted Carlson/Fotodynamics, cover, 6, 12, 19
Photo courtesy of General Dynamics Land Systems, 5, 16–17, 20–21
United Defense, L.P., 29
U.S. Marine Corps photo by Sergeant Paul L. Anstine II, 11

1 2 3 4 5 6 09 08 07 06 05 04

Table of Contents

CHAPTER 1

The M1A1 in Action

In an enemy country, 14 U.S. Army M1A1 Abrams tanks are undercover at the edge of a small wooded area. The tanks' long main guns poke through the trees. In the distance, the tanks' crew members see a large cloud of dust. As the dust settles, they see enemy tanks approaching.

As the enemy tanks get closer, the U.S. M1A1 crews aim at their targets. They fire their main guns when the enemy tanks are about 1 mile (1.6 kilometers) away. Within seconds, twelve enemy tanks grind to a halt and burn. The remaining enemy tank crews fire back. Bullets hit two M1A1s. But the bullets fail to go through the tanks' strong armor.

The M1A1 Abrams is one of the world's most powerful tanks.

LEARN ABOUT:

M1A1 history

M1A1 features

Recent M1A1 missions

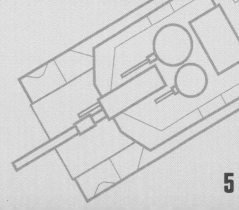

As the battle continues, the enemy tank crews suffer heavy losses. The enemy commander orders a retreat. The tank crews turn around and return to their bases.

The M1A1 has been in service since the mid-1980s.

Building the M1A1

In the mid-1980s, the U.S. Army wanted an updated model of its M1 Abrams tank. The Army had been using the M1 since 1981.

Between 1985 and 1993, General Dynamics Land Systems (GDLS) built about 4,500 new tanks for the Army. They were called M1A1s. The company also built about 200 M1A1s for the U.S. Marine Corps. Today, the Army and Marine Corps have a total of about 5,000 M1A1s.

The M1A1 has several improvements over the M1. Its main gun is more powerful. The M1A1 also has stronger armor than the M1. The armor protects M1A1 crews from enemy attacks. A better suspension system of springs and shock absorbers helps the M1A1 travel over rough ground.

About the M1A1

The M1A1 is one of the world's most advanced tanks. M1A1 tanks have helped crews survive heavy fighting in combat. In 1991, Operation Desert Storm began after Iraq invaded the neighboring country of Kuwait. The U.S. military went to Kuwait to force the Iraqi troops from the country. By the end of the war, about 2,000 M1A1s had destroyed nearly 2,600 Iraqi armored fighting vehicles. No M1A1s were destroyed by weapons from Iraqi tanks.

In 2003, the United States led Operation Iraqi Freedom. The United States and Great Britain invaded Iraq. Dozens of M1A1 tank crews helped take over Iraq's capital, Baghdad.

In 2003, M1A1 tank crews played a major role in Operation Iraqi Freedom.

CHAPTER 2

Inside the M1A1

The M1A1 Abrams is large and heavy. It is 12 feet (3.7 meters) high and 8 feet (2.4 meters) wide. It is 32 feet (9.8 meters) long with the main gun extended forward. It weighs about 68 tons (62 metric tons).

The M1A1's large size allows it to carry a variety of weapons and equipment. It has a large main gun and three smaller guns. The M1A1 stores ammunition called rounds. The tank crew fires the rounds from the guns. The M1A1 also has advanced electronic systems.

M1A1 Hull

The main body of the M1A1 is the hull. The hull supports the other parts of the tank. A rotating structure called a turret is attached to the top of the hull. Road wheels are mounted underneath the hull. Large tracks wrap around the road wheels.

The hull protects the crew and supports the rotating turret.

LEARN ABOUT:

M1A1 armor

Crew duties

M1A1 electronics

The outside of the M1A1's hull is made of strong, layered armor. The Army's early tanks had one layer of steel armor. In the 1970s, some of the world's militaries began to use high-explosive antitank (HEAT) rounds. The rounds could easily pass through steel. The layered armor on the M1A1 is made of a combination of materials. The materials are designed to stop HEAT rounds.

Crew members fire guns from the M1A1's turret.

Turret

The M1A1 turret holds some of the tank's most important equipment. It contains the main gun and seats for crew members. The rear of the turret holds ammunition. Smoke grenade dischargers are located on each side of the turret. The smoke produced by the grenades hides the tank from enemy forces.

Some M1A1 turrets have a layer of depleted uranium (DU) armor. The DU armor is underneath a layer of steel. DU is heavier than steel. The armor helps keep enemy ammunition from going through the turret. Tanks equipped with DU armor are called M1A1 Heavy Armor (HA) tanks.

Engine

The M1A1 has an AGT-1500 engine in the rear of the hull. The engine provides power to make the road wheels turn. The engine gives the M1A1 a top speed of about 45 miles (72 kilometers) per hour on smooth roads.

The AGT-1500 is a gas turbine engine. Gas turbine engines provide a great deal of power for their size. They also are quiet. Some militaries call the M1A1 the "whispering death."

Crew

Four crew members sit inside the M1A1. These crew members are the vehicle commander, driver, gunner, and loader.

The M1A1 vehicle commander is in charge of the tank crew. The commander sits at the rear of the turret. Six viewing devices called periscopes allow the commander to see outside the tank. The commander also can look through a weapon sight to see targets.

The driver controls the tank's movement from a seat near the hull's front. The driver looks through one of three periscopes.

The gunner aims and fires the tank's main gun from a seat in front of the commander. The gunner looks through a weapon sight.

The loader sits across from the vehicle commander and gunner. The loader keeps the guns supplied with ammunition.

Electronic Equipment

The M1A1 has advanced electronic equipment. Much of this equipment allows the crew members to see at night, through smoke, and during bad weather conditions.

At night, the driver can replace one of the periscopes with a passive night sight. This device collects and uses light from the moon and stars. It forms a picture of the tank's path on a screen.

The gunner's weapon sight has a thermal imaging system (TIS). The TIS allows the gunner to see targets in daylight and darkness. It senses heat in objects. The objects then appear on the sight's eyepiece.

Other electronic systems protect the M1A1. A fire suppression system helps prevent fires inside the tank. Another system protects the crew if enemy forces release dangerous chemicals into the air.

M1A1 crew members can open hatches above them to look outside the tank.

The M1A1

Function:	Main Battle Tank
Manufacturer:	General Dynamics Land Systems Inc.
Date First Deployed:	1985
Length (main gun forward):	32 feet (9.8 meters)
Height:	8 feet (2.4 meters)
Width:	12 feet (3.7 meters)
Weight (fully loaded):	68.4 tons (62 metric tons)
Engine:	AGT-1500 turbine engine
Main Gun Range:	2 miles (3.2 kilometers)
Top Road Speed:	45 miles (72 kilometers) per hour
Top Off-Road Speed:	30 miles (48 kilometers) per hour
Top Range:	289 miles (465 kilometers)
Fuel Capacity:	505.3 gallons (1,913 liters)

1 M256 main gun

2 Turret

3 Smoke grenade dischargers

4 Track

5 Road wheels

6 M2 machine gun

7 M240 machine gun

8 Hull

CHAPTER 3

Weapons and Tactics

The M1A1 is designed to destroy enemy tanks and other ground vehicles. The tank's main gun fires a round that can punch a hole in even the most heavily armored targets. The M1A1's machine guns can destroy unarmored or lightly armored targets.

Main Gun

The 120-millimeter (mm) M256 main gun was designed in Germany. The gun weighs 2,590 pounds (1,175 kilograms). It has a range of about 2 miles (3.2 kilometers).

LEARN ABOUT:

The M1A1's guns
KE rounds
HEAT rounds

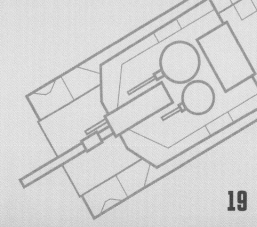

The M256 has a fire control system. This system includes a computer that automatically adjusts the main gun's position. The computer then keeps the gun stable. The gun remains locked on a target even as the tank travels over rough ground.

A fire control system keeps the main gun stable as it fires powerful rounds.

The gunner can use the main gun's laser range finder to learn the distance to a target. The laser shoots a beam of light at a target. The range then appears on the gunner's weapon sight.

Machine Guns

A 7.62 mm M240 machine gun moves with the main gun. The gunner fires the M240. The gun has a top range of about .5 mile (.8 kilometer).

Other machine guns move separately from the main gun. A Browning M2 .50-caliber gun is located above the commander's seat. The M2 .50 has a top range of about 1 mile (1.6 kilometers). Another 7.62 mm M240 machine gun is above the loader's seat.

Main Gun Ammunition

The M1A1 carries 40 rounds for the main gun. These rounds can be one of several types. The M829A2 kinetic energy (KE) round is the most common. Tank crews sometimes call KE rounds sabot rounds or "silver bullets." They travel faster than 1 mile (1.6 kilometers) per second. KE rounds can easily punch a hole through tank armor.

KE rounds are in a case called a sabot. The sabot is made of carbon and other materials. It falls away shortly after the round leaves the main gun.

HEAT rounds are another type of main gun ammunition. These rounds have a warhead that explodes when it hits a target. The M1A1 currently uses the M830 HEAT round. Eventually, all M830s will be replaced with M830A1s. Like KE rounds, M830A1s have a sabot. They also have a sensor that allows them to destroy enemy helicopters.

M1A1 crews often use main gun rounds during training exercises.

Formations and Tactics

On missions, M1A1 tanks form groups called units. The smallest unit is the four-tank platoon. The largest unit is a division. A division has about 300 tanks and 15,000 soldiers.

When M1A1 crews go into battle, they make different formations. Formations include the line, echelon, and wedge.

In the line formation, tanks line up side by side. This formation is best for frontal attacks. It lessens the risk of M1A1 tanks being hit by rounds from their own unit.

In the echelon, tanks form an angled line. The echelon allows tanks to easily fire to the front and to one side.

The wedge formation is the combination of a left and right echelon. It creates a *V* in front of the target area. The wedge provides good protection from enemy forces on all sides.

M1A1 Formations

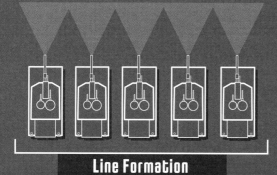

Line Formation

Echelon Formation

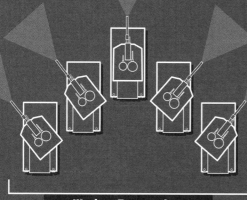

Wedge Formation

CHAPTER 4

The Future

Military officials plan to keep the M1A1 Abrams as its main tank until at least 2016. The tank has proven its usefulness in recent conflicts and wars. The Army wants to make sure it remains one of the world's best tanks.

M1A1 Improvements

The Army has regularly updated the M1A1 since it entered service. In 1999, the Army began rebuilding 2,000 M1A1s. This project is called the Abrams Integrated Management (AIM) Overhaul program. The rebuilt tanks will have advanced digital systems. These systems will help tank crews keep track of their surroundings. The Army expects to complete the program in about 2012.

Tank crews showed the M1A1's abilities during Operation Iraqi Freedom.

LEARN ABOUT:

AIM Overhaul program

The M1A2 SEP

Future Combat Systems

In the early 2000s, the Army hired companies to develop a new engine for the M1A1. This engine is the LV100-5. The engine has fewer parts and uses less fuel than the AGT-1500.

The M1A2

In 1989, General Dynamics Land Systems began producing M1A2s for the Army. The company completed 62 M1A2s by 1992. Later, the Army decided to update its older tanks rather than build new tanks. Between 1993 and 2001, GDLS updated more than 1,000 M1s to M1A2 standards.

M1A2s are equipped with a Commander's Independent Thermal Viewer (CITV). The CITV works like the gunner's thermal imaging system. But the CITV allows an M1A2 crew to aim at more than one target faster than an M1A1 tank crew. The gunner can shoot at one target. At the same time, the commander can use the CITV to look for the next target.

In 2001, GDLS began upgrading M1A2s as part of a program called the M1A2 System Enhancement Package (SEP). The M1A2 SEP will have improved thermal sights. The Army plans to complete SEP upgrades for about 1,000 M1A2s by 2012.

Future Plans

After Abrams tanks are retired, the Army may replace them with vehicles equipped with Future Combat Systems (FCSs). FCS vehicles are in the early stages of development. The vehicles' communication, control, and command systems will use advanced equipment.

Abrams tanks have played a major role in the Army and Marines for several years. The firepower and defense systems of both M1A1s and M1A2s will continue to be a threat to other militaries throughout the world.

FCS vehicles may replace M1A1s.

Glossary

ammunition (am-yuh-NISH-uhn)—rounds, missiles, and other objects that can be fired from weapons

armor (AR-mur)—a protective metal covering

hull (HUL)—the outside structure of a tank that supports the other tank parts

periscope (PER-uh-skope)—a viewing device with mirrors at each end; tank crew members use periscopes to view their surroundings while staying inside the tank.

platoon (pluh-TOON)—a group of tanks that work together during training and in battles

range (RAYNJ)—the maximum distance ammunition can travel to reach its target or the distance that a vehicle can travel without refueling

road wheel (ROHD WEEL)—a large, heavy wheel that connects the track to the tank

round (ROUND)—a single bullet fired by a gun

sabot (sah-BOH)—a case that holds a round and fills up the extra space inside a gun's barrel

turret (TUR-it)—a rotating structure on top of a tank that holds the main gun

warhead (WOR-hed)—the explosive part of ammunition

Read More

Bartlett, Richard. *U.S. Army Fighting Vehicles.* U.S. Armed Forces. Chicago: Heinemann Library, 2003.

Black, Michael A. *Tanks: The M1A1 Abrams.* High-Tech Military Weapons. New York: Children's Press, 2000.

Sievert, Terri. *The U.S. Army at War.* On the Front Lines. Mankato, Minn.: Capstone Press, 2002.

Useful Addresses

U.S. Army Public Affairs
Office of the Chief of Public Affairs
1500 Army Pentagon
Washington, DC 20310-1500

U.S. Army Tank-Automotive and Armaments Command (TACOM)
Attn.: AMSTA-CP-PI (History)/MS 432
6501 East 11 Mile Road
Warren, MI 48397-5000

Internet Sites

FactHound offers a safe, fun way to find Internet sites related to this book. All of the sites on FactHound have been researched by our staff.

Here's how:

1. Visit *www.facthound.com*
2. Type in this special code **0736824162** for age-appropriate sites. Or enter a search word related to this book for a more general search.
3. Click on the **Fetch It** button.

FactHound will fetch the best sites for you!

Index